Volume 8
Decodable
Reader

Mc
Graw
Hill
Education

Bothell, WA • Chicago, IL • Columbus, OH • New York, NY

Contents

Good Pets

by Lucas Reed

illustrated by Karen Tafoya

Snookie and Cookie are a cat and a dog. They are good pets.

Let's look at Snookie and Cookie. We can find out more about these pets.

Some pets like to nap in the warm sun.
Some are happy napping in little spaces.
Snookie rests on a wool rug in the
sunshine. Cookie naps in a nook in the
bookcase.

When it is warm, pets like to go out.
If it gets too hot, they shed some fur.
Look at Snookie and Cookie. They
shook some of their fur off!

If you wore a coat and got too hot,
you would take it off!

When it is hot, your pet might eat less. The meal may be good, but pets might not feel like eating much.

You shouldn't be too concerned. Pets stop eating when they feel full.

Snookie and Cookie nap when it's hot.
Cookie naps in the shadow of a pot.
Snookie takes a chilly dip in the brook.

If you put your foot in a brook on a
hot day, it would feel nice.

Snookie and Cookie find shady places.
Snookie hides under a wood porch.
Cookie gets shade under a toy car hood.

They couldn't wait to go inside! They
stood by the fan for awhile.

Now we know more about these
pets. Look at them nap. They
are good friends and good pets.

8

Under the MOON

by Antonio Jenkins
illustrated by Brenda Johnson

Under the moon, an owl begins to stir. In the gloom of night, it hoots its lonely tune, "Whoo? Whoo? Who are you?"

A bird swoops down to eat a tasty snack. A bat hunts for food. Tiny mice hide in the grass.

Under the moon, cows moo and then take a snooze. Soon, five sheep in fluffy suits close their eyes. They all sleep on the grass wet with dew.

Under the moon, a loon and her new baby float on the smooth lake. The night is cool and dark, but the moon sheds light on the loons as they swim.

Under the moon, a moose munches leaves on a forest path. A snake hisses at the moose and then slithers under a tree root for some rest.

Under the moon, three chipmunks
in a goofy mood play on a roof.
The chipmunks chatter as they
chew their food.

Under the moon, fox cubs play.
A bird chirps and coos as she
snoops on them.

Now, the sun begins to rise. Rays of bright sunlight shoot across the blue sky. A new July day will begin soon.

Paul's Turn

by Caleb Wilson

illustrated by Barry Mullins

Gramps likes to draw. Paul likes to paint. They enjoy talking about art. First, Gramps draws a hawk. Paul watches.

"What color will you paint the hawk?" Gramps asks.

"I saw a hawk last August," Paul tells Gramps. He thinks about the hawk. "It had strong wings and mighty claws. It was brown!"

Paul paints the hawk brown. Now, Gramps draws a home with a lawn.

"That's my house," remarks Paul. He thinks about his home and yard. "I like to walk barefoot on the lawn. Sometimes I crawl on the soft green grass!"

Paul paints the lawn green. Gramps draws the sun rising at dawn.

"When the sun begins to rise, it's dawn," explains Paul. He thinks about the sun rising. "I woke up at dawn once. The sky was splashed with red!"

Paul paints the sky red. Gramps draws a pumpkin.

"I saw a pumpkin last week," says Paul. He thinks about the pumpkin patch. "The pumpkin was orange. It was on top of straw. The straw was yellow!"

Paul paints the pumpkin and straw. Mom walks in. Gramps draws her.

"That's Mom in a shawl!" exclaims Paul.
Paul paints Mom in her blue shawl.
"I see that Gramps showed you how to
paint. He showed me how to paint
when I was small," grins Mom.

"I know," smiles Paul. "And now it's
my turn!"

Walt Ought to Clean Up

by Evan Myers

illustrated by Barbara Counseller

Walt never thought he ought to clean his room.

"I like my room this way," he thought.

But Walt's family did not agree. They thought Walt ought to clean up. Walt couldn't even get to his bed without walking over piles.

Even if he wanted a clean room, where would he start? His room was filled with all kinds of things that Walt bought. There were piles of clothes everywhere.

"I'm sure this is just a phase for Walt," Mom explained.

But Dad and Roy disagreed. They decided that Walt's room was a major mess! Walt ought to clean it up.

Roy had a thought.

"I would like to challenge you to a contest. If you win, your room can stay a mess," Roy explained. "But if I win," Roy went on, "you will have to clean up the mess."

Walt thought about it. He enjoyed contests. And he really liked to win!

Walt and Roy gripped hands. Then they fought using their arms.

"I will win," Walt thought.

"Walt will be taught a lesson," Roy thought.

Walt and Roy stared at each other.

Roy did not budge. Walt did not budge. Then Walt's wrist hit the desk. Walt lost the contest.

Walt had to clean his room!

Walt brought Roy into his room. Roy couldn't believe his eyes.

"I thought I liked messes," said Walt. "But you taught me. A clean room really is the best."

A Pleasant Visit

by Christine Wilson

illustrated by Francisco Rodriguez

"Sydney, I need you to take some things down the road to Grandma," Mom said.

"I just ate breakfast. Can I go later?" Sydney asked.

"Go soon. The forecast calls for rain," said Mom.

Young Sydney looked at Mom.

Mom explained to her daughter,
"Grandma's house is easy to get to.
Take Egypt with you. It will be fun."

Mom packed supplies for Grandma.

Sydney dreaded carrying the heavy
bag. But the bag was not heavy.
It was light. Her gym class had
made her strong!

Sydney and Egypt headed to
Grandma's house.

Her feet made a nice rhythm as
she marched down the path.

Clip, clop, flip, flop, stamp, stomp.

The weather was rainy and gloomy.
But soon they were at Grandma's
house. Sydney walked in ahead of
Egypt. She almost tripped on the rug.

Blip, blop, clip, clop, flip, flop, flick,
flock, click, clock, drip, drop.

The sun began to shine as soon as Sydney entered the house. The rays warmed the room. Then Sydney spotted Grandma.

"Grandma!" Sydney exclaimed. "I am so happy to see you."

"I'm happy to see you too. Are you hungry? I made a couple of sandwiches on my homemade bread. Let's eat," said Grandma.

Sydney and Grandma ate lunch. They had a long pleasant visit.

Mee-Ling's Mission

by Jennifer Li
illustrated by Stephanie Pershing

Mee-Ling lived in a small village.
The land was rough and dry. It had
not rained for a long time. The
villagers' crops were not growing.
There was not enough water.

A dragon lived at the top of the mountain. "Do not go near the dragon!" people would say.

But Mee-Ling thought, "Is that dragon scaring the water away?"

She had to find out. She explained to her parents, "I have a mission, a job, to do. I must ask the dragon for rain. I assure you it is our only hope."

"It's too dangerous!" her parents called. But Mee-Ling was on her way and misheard her parents' call.

Mee-Ling walked on. The dragon was awake. Red-hot stones shot angrily from its mouth. It was like a stone-throwing machine. Mee-Ling swiftly ducked behind a huge rock.

Mee-Ling reached the top. She heard the dragon sing. "Alone I live. Alone I cry. I am friendless and sad, oh my!"

Mee-Ling said, "Nonsense, don't feel lonely! My village needs you."

The dragon breathed in. Mee-Ling didn't know if it was a laugh or cough!

The dragon explained, "No one has ever visited. I thought I'd never have a pal."

"Come," Mee-Ling said. "Be my pal."

Together, they headed back. On the way, there was an amazing development. The dragon's tail cut into the mountain. Cool water began to flow.

Forever after, a river flowed. It followed the dragon's path through the town. Crops had water. Plants began to grow. The village chefs made a feast. Mee-Ling and the dragon were heroes!

Volume 8

Decodable Words

Target Phonics Elements: Variant Vowel: /u̇/ *oo, ou, u*
brook, Cookie, couldn't, foot, full, good, hood, look, nook, put, shook, shouldn't, stood, wood, wool

High-Frequency Words

Review: *are, do, of, some, their, to, too, warm, you, your*

Story Words
friends

Decodable Words

Target Phonics Elements: Variant Vowel: /ü/ *oo, u, u_e, ew, ue, ui*
blue, chew, cool, coos, dew, food, gloom, goofy, hoots, July, moo, moon, moose, new, roof, root, shoot, soon, smooth, snoops, swoops, suit, whoo, woops

High-Frequency Words

Review: *are, of, their, who, you*

Story Words
eyes

Decodable Words
Target Phonics Elements: Variant Vowel /ô/ a, aw, au, al
August, claw, crawl, dawn, draw, lawn, Paul, saw, shawl, small, straw, talking, walk

High-Frequency Words
Review: *of, once, says to, was*, you

Story Words
orange

Decodable Words
Target Phonics Elements: Variant Vowel /ô/ augh, ough
bought, brought, fought, ought, taught

High-Frequency Words
Review: *have, into, of, other, sure, their, to, were, you, your*

Story Words
eyes

Decoding skills taught to date:

Phonics: Short *a*; Short *i*; Short *o*; Short *e*, Short *u*; *l*- Blends; *r*- Blends; *s* -Blends; end Blends; Long *a: a_e*; Long *i: i_e*; Long *o: o_e*; Long u: *u_e*; Soft *c*, Soft *g* ,-*dge*; Consonant Digraphs: *th, sh, -ng*; Consonant Digraphs: *ch, -tch, wh, ph*; Three-Letter Blends; Long *a: ai, ay*; Long *i: i, igh, ie, y*; Long *o: o, ow, oa, oe*; Long *e: e_e, ee, ea, e, ie*; Long *e: y, ey*; Long *u: u_e, ew, u, ue, /ûr/: er, ir, ur, or; /är/ ar; /ôr/ or, oar, ore; /îr/ eer, ere, ear; /âr/ are, air, ear, ere*; Long *a: a, ea, ei, ey*; Silent Letters: *wr, kn, gn, mb, sc;* Silent Letters: *rh, gh, bt, mn, lf, lk, st;* Diphthongs: *ou, ow;* Diphthongs: *oi, oy;* Variant Vowel: */u̇/ oo, ou, u;* Variant Vowel: */ü/ oo, u, u_e, ew, ue, ui;* Variant Vowel: */ô/ a, aw, au, al;* Variant Vowel: */ô/ augh, ough;* Short Vowel Digraphs: */e/ea, /u/ou, /i/y;* Consonant Digraphs: */f/gh, /sh/ch, ss*

Structural Analysis: Plural Nouns *-s;* Inflectional Ending *-s;* Plural Nouns *-es;* Inflectional ending *-es;* Closed Syllables; Inflectional Ending *-ed;* Inflectional Ending *-ing;* Possessives (singular); Inflectional Endings *-ed, -ing* (drop finale e); Inflectional Endings *-ed, -ing* (double final consonant); CVCe Syllables; Prefixes *re-, un-, dis-;* Suffixes *-ful, -less;* Compound Words; Contractions with *'s, 're, 'll, 've;* Open Syllables; Contractions with *not (isn't, aren't, wasn't, weren't, hasn't, haven't, can't);* Inflectional Endings and Plurals (change *y* to *i*); Comparative Inflectional endings *-er, -est;* Irregular Plurals; Abbreviations; *r*-Controlled Syllables; Plural Possessives, Prefixes *pre-, non-, mis-;* Consonant +*le* Syllables (+*le, +al, +el*); Contractions with *not (wouldn't, couldn't, shouldn't);* Vowel Team Syllables, Suffixes *-y, -ly*